I0418523

# B.E.T.T.E.R²

## THE 7 PILLARS OF PERSONAL REINVENTION

### SYLVESTER MAYO

**B.E.T.T.E.R.²: The Seven Pillars of Reinvention**
Published by JM Publishing, LLC
New York, New York, U.S.A.
www.jmpublishingllc.com

Copyright © 2025 by Sylvester Mayo. All rights reserved.
ISBN: 979-8-9893196-2-6 (paperback)

No part of this publication may be reproduced, stored in a retrieval system, or transmitted in any form or by any means, electronic, mechanical, photocopying, recording, or otherwise, without prior written permission from the publisher or the author, except by a reviewer who may quote brief passages in a review.

The publisher and the author do not make any guarantee or promise regarding any results that may be obtained through the use of the content of this book. You should never make any financial, business, or investment decision without first consulting your own professional advisor and conducting thorough research and due diligence.

To the maximum extent permitted by law, the publisher and the author disclaim any liability for any loss, negative outcome, or damages arising from the use of, reliance on, or interpretation of any information, commentary, analysis, advice, or recommendations contained in this book.

All images, logos, quotes, and trademarks included in this publication are used in accordance with all applicable trademark and copyright laws of the United States of America.

**Quantity Purchases:**
Schools, companies, professional groups, clubs, and other organizations may qualify for special terms when ordering multiple copies of this title. For more information, please email **info@sylvestermayo.com**.

All rights reserved by Sylvester Mayo and JM Publishing, LLC.
Printed in the United States of America.

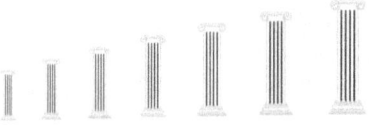

# CONTENTS

# DEDICATION

I humbly dedicate this book to Almighty God, whose divine inspiration, wisdom, and insight have guided my life and shaped my journey toward becoming better.

In loving memory of my maternal grandfather, John Jasper Mayo, you provided a safe place for me to grow, to learn, and to become. Your words always spoke life, possibility, and purpose into my spirit. Your legacy continues to live through me.

To my loving wife, Arlene, your steadfastness, loyalty, and unwavering consistency over more than 40 years have transformed the trajectory of my life. I am forever grateful for your love. And to my children, Lee, Ebony, Jeremy, Robert, and Whitney—you are my blessings, my inspiration, and the laughter that sustains me.

To my spiritual mother, Dr. E. Lorraine Langham, thank you for being a steady force in my development. Your guidance, prayers, and wisdom have shaped my growth in more ways than words can express.

And to the countless leaders, friends, colleagues, and acquaintances who have shared moments of insight, truth, and experience, thank you. Your voices, lessons, and presence have all contributed to the creation of this book. This work is, in many ways, the culmination of our collective learnings.

# INTRODUCTION

Every person reaches a moment when the life they are living no longer matches the life they desire. Sometimes this realization arrives quietly, a gentle pull reminding you that you were created for more. At other times it comes through heartbreak, loss, disappointment, or a storm that shook you so deeply that you can no longer pretend everything is fine. Maybe you lost someone you loved, the relationship you prayed for would last, the business you invested your heart into, the confidence you once carried, or the version of yourself you always imagined you would become. Maybe you are waking up every day feeling stuck, tired of repeating the same cycles, tired of surviving instead of thriving, tired of wanting better love, better relationships, better finances, better opportunities, better habits, better health, better peace, and better time with the people who matter most.

The truth is simple. Most people are not broken. They are buried. Buried under fear, under disappointment, under responsibility, under the weight of their past, and under the pressure to be strong when they feel anything but strong. They are not damaged beyond repair. Their potential is not gone. Their purpose is not lost. Their strength is not missing. It is simply hidden beneath the layers of pain, pressure, expectations, and survival that life has placed on top of them. When the weight begins to lift, the real you is revealed. The part of you that still believes, still hopes, still dreams, and still has the power to rise. You are not broken. You are buried. And buried things can rise again.

When you understand that you are buried and not broken, you can finally begin the sacred work of rising. This is where the *B.E.T.T.E.R²* framework becomes essential. Becoming better is not about perfection. It is about direction. It is the daily decision to rise above your circumstances, your excuses, and your old identity. This book exists to guide you toward the better version of yourself through a simple and powerful system called *B.E.T.T.E.R²*, a framework created to elevate your life from the inside out. Better begins with defining success for yourself, identifying what you want to improve, and being honest about the areas of your life that need elevation. The seven principles you are about to learn,

Belief, Energy, Talent, Time, Enlist, Read and Reinvention, may seem simple, but when they are practiced with consistency and sincerity, they have the power to restore clarity, rebuild confidence, reignite purpose, and transform your entire life.

Everything begins with belief, because nothing in your life improves until you believe that improvement is possible. Your energy must align with the life you want to live, because your attitude, your discipline, and your emotional strength shape every result you experience. Your talent must be developed, sharpened, and used with intention. Your time must be respected and invested wisely. You must enlist the right people, because growth requires community, mentorship, and accountability. And your future must be strengthened through reading, because knowledge expands your mind, deepens your wisdom, and opens the door to new opportunities.

Even if you feel lost, you are not defeated. Even if you feel stuck, you are not finished. Even if you feel empty, this is the exact place where a new version of you can rise. You do not have to remain where life left you. You have the power to stand up, to grow, to rebuild, and to become better. Better is not something you chase. Better is something you become. It is already present within you, waiting for awareness, waiting for permission, waiting for you to uncover what life attempted to hide. Better is the part of you that fear tried to silence and the part of you that pain tried to bury. It has never left you. It has only been covered by the weight of your experiences. Through your belief, your energy, your talent, your time, the people you enlist, and the wisdom you read and absorb, you will awaken the strength, the clarity, and the potential that have lived inside you all along. *B.E.T.T.E.R²* is both your identity and your evolution. *B.E.T.T.E.R²* is who you are at your core and who you are called to become with intention. *B.E.T.T.E.R²* does not require pursuit. *B.E.T.T.E.R²* requires awareness, acceptance, and action. *B.E.T.T.E.R²* begins now. *B.E.T.T.E.R²* begins within. *B.E.T.T.E.R²* begins the moment you decide to stop chasing and start becoming.

*"Your life does not rise when your circumstances change; it rises the moment your belief changes."* — *Sylvester Mayo*

# CHAPTER ONE

# BELIEF

## The First Pillar of Personal Reinvention

*Your life cannot rise until your belief rises. Every transformation begins with the courage to believe something new about yourself." — Sylvester Mayo*

One of the simplest stories in childhood carries one of the greatest truths for adulthood. There was a small engine assigned to simple work in a rail yard. It moved cars back and forth, assisted with short tasks, and was never expected to do more than its usual routine. Near the yard stood larger, stronger, more powerful engines that were built for heavy loads and long-distance hauls.

One day, a long line of freight cars needed to be taken over a steep hill. The train asked the largest engine to take it across, but the engine refused. It claimed the load was too heavy and the climb was too demanding. The train asked another engine, and then another, only to hear excuses, hesitation, and the familiar language of self-doubt.

In desperation, the train turned to the smallest engine in the yard, the one no one believed was capable. The task was far beyond its size, its record, and its reputation. Yet when the request was made, the little engine did not evaluate the weight of the freight or the height of the hill. It evaluated its belief. It simply said, "I think I can."

That quiet decision changed everything.

The small engine positioned itself at the front of the massive train. As it started climbing, the hill pushed against it, the weight resisted it, and the path grew steeper. Every larger engine had quit at this point. Every stronger engine had refused the challenge. But the small engine kept affirming its belief with every turn of its wheels: "I think I can, I think I can."

As it approached the steepest part of the climb, it slowed down. The struggle became real. The effort became exhausting. Yet the belief did not change. Through persistence, courage, and steady focus, it reached the top of the hill that was supposed to break it. On the other side, it moved with confidence, declaring, "I thought I could."

The little engine did not succeed because it was the biggest or the strongest. It succeeded because it believed. Belief carried it where strength alone could not. And the same is true for you. Before anything becomes possible in your life, it must first become believable. That story reveals a deeper truth: belief is the internal force that shapes everything you do.

Belief is not a word. Belief is a system. Belief is a pattern. Belief is a lens. Belief is the button that turns the engine of your life on or off. And since belief shapes your life, you must understand where your beliefs come from. Before any transformation begins, you must ask yourself a powerful and uncomfortable question: What do you truly believe about yourself? Not what you tell people. Not what you pretend to feel. Not what you wish you believed. What do you genuinely believe at your core?

Because your belief systems are not accidents. They are shaped by two things: your internal world or your external world. One of the clearest ways to see this in everyday life is through the difference between external blame and internal ownership.

If your belief is controlled by the outside world, your confidence will rise and fall based on circumstances. You will believe in yourself when life approves of you and doubt yourself when life challenges you. This is the external locus of control. It creates a life full of excuses, justifications, and blame. If you have ever been to a bowling alley, you may have seen how this works. One person throws the ball into the gutter and immediately complains. The lanes were not oiled. The ball did not fit. The shoes were uncomfortable. The people next to them were distracting. Everything becomes the reason they did not succeed, except themselves.

External belief systems weaken you. They convince you that you are powerless. They convince you that life is happening to you. They convince you that success belongs to someone else and that failure is always someone else's fault. The problem with external belief is simple. When excuses increase, growth stops.

Internal belief is different. Internal belief is ownership. Internal belief is accountability. Internal belief is agency. Internal belief says, "If I want to be successful, it is up to me." There was a time I was at the bowling alley, and while the atmosphere was competitive, my final score was an 88. My focus was not on the number. My focus was on the moment. The bumper pads were up, the laughter was real, the smiles were effortless, and the memories became far more important than the scoreboard. I owned the experience. I owned the joy. I owned the outcome. That is the internal locus of control. It says, "I am the captain of my own fate. I am responsible for my direction. I decide how I show up. I decide how I respond. I decide who I become."

When the shift is made from external control to internal control, life changes instantly. Because belief becomes a choice and not a reaction. Psychology supports this truth and explains exactly why belief has so much influence.

Psychology gives us a powerful truth about belief. It is called Cognitive Behavioral Therapy. Cognitive Behavioral Therapy teaches that your thoughts shape your emotions, your emotions shape your behavior, and your behavior shapes your results. Many people try to change their behavior without changing the thoughts that created the behavior. But you cannot change what you do until you change what you think.

If you think you are not capable, your behavior will match that belief.

If you think you are unworthy, your behavior will reflect that belief.

If you think you cannot grow, you will not grow.

CBT teaches that if you want a better life, you must first learn to think differently. Thinking differently is the root of believing differently. And believing differently is the beginning of becoming better. One of the most effective ways to train new thoughts is to slow them down long enough for you to examine them. And few tools do that better than journaling.

Journaling becomes one of the most powerful tools in this process. When you place your thoughts on paper, you slow your mind long enough to see what has been shaping your belief. Thoughts that once felt heavy begin to lose their strength. You can examine them with honesty, challenge them with clarity, and replace them with intention. A journal becomes the space where you meet your true self. You cannot rewrite a story you refuse to read. You cannot heal a belief you refuse to face. Journaling helps you reveal the thoughts that have been directing your identity, and it gives you the authority to decide which ones remain and which ones must be released.

If you do not like the thoughts you are thinking, you must learn to substitute them. Write them down so you can see them. Then, replace fear with faith. Replace doubt with possibility. Replace excuses with action. Replace limitation with curiosity. This process of replacing thoughts is how belief grows stronger day by day.

Growth requires new thoughts. New thoughts become new beliefs. And new beliefs become a new life.

## What YOU Believe about YOU Shapes Who YOU Become

Belief does not only influence how you think. Belief influences who you think you are. Every action you take, every risk you avoid, every opportunity you accept, and every limitation you surrender to is connected to your identity. Identity is the blueprint of your life. It is the silent architect shaping your decisions long before you consciously make them.

People do not struggle because they lack potential. They struggle because they adopt an identity that convinces them they cannot rise. An identity formed in childhood. An identity shaped by environments. An identity weakened by disappointment. An identity buried beneath rejection, comparison, or the pressure to survive. Without realizing it, many people are living today through beliefs they accepted years ago.

Identity speaks in quiet sentences:

"This is just who I am."
"I do not deserve more."
"I have always been this way."
"People like me do not succeed."
"I cannot change."

These beliefs do not shout, yet they control everything. They become invisible rules that determine the size of your life. When you try to rise, they pull you back. When you reach for more, they remind you of less. When you attempt change, they whisper the old story.

But identity is not permanent. Identity is programmable. When your belief changes, your identity begins to shift. You start to see yourself differently. You start to expect more from yourself. You start to challenge the limits you once accepted. You begin to step into the version of yourself that your past tried to bury.

The difference between a fixed identity and a growth identity is the difference between a life that repeats itself and a life that evolves. A fixed identity says you are who you have been. A growth identity says you can become who you choose to be. A fixed identity looks backward. A growth identity looks forward. A fixed identity protects comfort. A growth identity pursues potential.

> *Understanding identity opens the door*
> *to the deeper work of belief, because you*
> *cannot rise until you confront the stories*
> *that taught you how to see yourself.*

Belief rewrites identity. And identity rewrites destiny.

Before you continue, ask yourself:
What identity have you been living in?
And is it lifting you or limiting you?

## How to Build A Stronger Belief and Rewrite The Stories That Broke it

Belief is not built in a moment. It is built over time. Day by day it is either taking us towards our goals and dreams or taking us away. When I was a child, adults taught us to say, "Sticks and stones may break my bones, but words will never hurt me." It sounded brave, but it was never true. Words do hurt. Words shape identity long before we understand identity. Words become beliefs long before we realize we accepted them. Many people grow up struggling to believe in themselves not because they lack ability, but because they were wounded by words spoken over them or spoken to themselves. Words become internal echoes. Echoes become beliefs. And beliefs become quiet limits that follow us for years.

I learned this early. Some of my peers and younger family members used to call me DT, short for Double Trouble. It was playful to them, but powerful to me. It was a label that tried to shape who I was supposed to be. But my grandfather saw something different in me. He never called me DT. He called me Young Professor. He spoke purpose, intelligence, and possibility over my life at a time when I did not yet understand the weight of identity. Out of the two names spoken over me, I chose the one that lifted me. I knew I was not trouble. I knew I was not defined by anyone's limitation or expectation. I believed I had meaning. I believed I would teach, guide, and empower. And that belief, planted through my grandfather's words, grew into the direction of my life. This is why belief matters. This is why identity matters. And this is why the words you hold onto matter even more.

Belief is built through daily practice, intentional thought, and the courage to confront the stories that shaped you. Every person carries an inner narrative. Every person walks through life repeating silent sentences formed from experiences, environments, and emotions. Some of these sentences strengthen you, but many of them limit you. If you want to build a stronger belief, you must learn both how to create new beliefs and how to release the old ones that have been weakening you for years.

Your belief grows through consistent intentional thinking. Your mind is always active, always processing, always interpreting. If you do not guide your thoughts, your thoughts will guide you. This is why so many people remain stuck in patterns that no longer serve them. Their beliefs are anchored to thoughts they never questioned and narratives they never challenged. Building belief requires you to slow down long enough to observe the thoughts that shape your life.

Earlier in this chapter we introduced journaling as a tool for thinking differently. Now we take it further, because journaling does more than reveal your thoughts. It helps you rewrite the stories that shaped your belief. This is where journaling becomes transformative. When you journal, you allow your thoughts to land on paper instead of circulating endlessly in your mind. Thoughts that once felt overwhelming begin to lose their power. You can see them clearly. You can question them honestly. You can replace them intentionally. A journal becomes the space where you meet your true self. You cannot rewrite a story you refuse to read. You cannot heal a belief you refuse to face. Journaling helps you reveal the thoughts that have been shaping your identity, and it gives you the authority to decide which ones remain.

Building belief also requires substitution. When a thought weakens you, you must replace it. Substitute fear with faith. Substitute doubt with possibility. Substitute excuses with responsibility. Substitute limitation with curiosity. You are not trying to silence the wrong thoughts. You are simply choosing stronger thoughts. And every time you do this, your belief strengthens. It takes practice, but every substitution is a step toward becoming the person you desire to be.

As we spoke about earlier, environment plays a role in this process. The people you speak to, the voices you listen to, the atmosphere you live in, and the conversations you give energy to all influence the strength of your belief. This starts as early as childhood. Belief is reinforced by community. When you spend time with people who aim higher, you begin to aim higher. When you surround yourself with people who challenge themselves, you challenge yourself. When you hear words that feed your growth, your inner voice becomes stronger. A healthy environment does not simply support belief. It protects it.

But to build a stronger belief, you must also confront the past. Every person carries stories that shaped their identity. Some were spoken by teachers, parents, partners, or peers.

Some were created during moments of failure. Some were built during seasons of survival. These stories feel true because they were repeated, but longevity does not equal truth. Many limiting beliefs were never accurate. They were simply accepted.

To move forward, you must recognize these stories and rewrite them. You are not rewriting history. You are rewriting interpretation. You are giving meaning to your past that empowers your future instead of limiting it. When you look back through the lens of growth, what once felt like failure becomes fuel. What once felt like rejection becomes redirection. What once felt like a wound becomes wisdom.

Old stories create fixed identities. New stories create growth identities. And your belief will always align with the story you believe most. You can tell yourself you are too late, or you can tell yourself you are right on time. You can tell yourself you are not enough, or you can tell yourself you are becoming more every day. You can tell yourself you cannot rise, or you can tell yourself you are rising now. The story does not change your life. The story changes you. And you change your life.

Belief is a daily practice. Belief is a conscious choice. Belief is a commitment to who you are becoming. As you build stronger thoughts, create supportive environments, substitute limiting beliefs, and rewrite old narratives, something powerful begins to happen. Identity shifts. Confidence rises. Vision expands. And the version of you that was once buried begins to come alive.

Before you close this chapter, pause and answer three questions that will shape everything that follows:

1. What belief have you been holding that no longer serves you?
2. What new belief must you practice daily to become the person you are meant to be?
3. What old story are you ready to rewrite so you can rise?

Because the life you want cannot grow in the soil of disbelief. It grows in the soil of belief that is strengthened every day by thought, practice, and truth. And today, your belief is rising.

## THE BELIEF PRACTICE (Action Steps)

Belief grows through repetition, intention, and awareness. These steps will help you begin strengthening your belief immediately and consistently.

### 1. Identify One Limiting Belief and Challenge It

Write down a belief that has been holding you back. Challenge it with one truth that empowers you. This is the beginning of rewriting the story that shaped your identity.

### 2. Replace One Weak Thought with One Strong Thought

Every time a limiting thought appears today, replace it with a stronger one. Substitution is the seed of transformation.

### 3. Create a Daily Belief Statement

Write one sentence that speaks to the person you are becoming. Repeat it every morning and every night. Your identity responds to the words you speak over your life.

## 4. Journal for Five Minutes Tonight

Return to the practice introduced earlier in this chapter. Let your thoughts land on paper. Clarity begins where honesty is written.

## 5. Remove One External Excuse

Choose one excuse that comes from outside yourself and release it. Replace it with internal ownership. Ownership strengthens belief.

## 6. Surround Yourself With One Source of Strength

Choose one source today that supports your growth. Your environment is the soil where belief grows.

## 7. Take One Small Action Toward the Person You Want To Become

Do something today that proves your belief to yourself. Belief expands when action supports it.

*"Your energy is the atmosphere of your life, and your life will always expand or shrink to match its temperature."* — *Sylvester Mayo*

# CHAPTER TWO

# ENERGY

**The Second Pillar of Personal Reinvention**

*"Your energy is the emotional temperature of
your life and your life can only rise to the level
you are willing to heat it."*
— *Sylvester Mayo*

Energy is one of the greatest forces in your life, yet most people never learn how to manage it, protect it, elevate it, or direct it. Before you speak, before you decide, before you plan, and before you act, your energy is already shaping the outcome. Your energy enters the room before you do. It communicates your belief, your confidence, your intentions, your fears, your direction, and your readiness without a single word being spoken. It influences the way people see you, the way opportunities approach you, and the way life responds to you. In the first pillar, we talked about belief, how belief determines what is possible for your life. Belief however alone is never enough. Belief sets the vision, energy sets the tone. Belief chooses the destination, energy determines the speed. Belief defines the dream, energy determines whether the dream ever becomes real.

Energy is your inner climate. It is your attitude in motion, your discipline expressed, your emotional strength revealed, and your focus applied. It is the current that guides your decisions, shapes your habits, and influences the way you navigate challenges. Two people can face the same setback with the same level of skill, the same tools, and the same opportunity yet one will rise while the other collapses. The difference is not the obstacle but the energy behind the response. One uses adversity to grow; the other uses adversity to shrink. Energy decides the direction.

Most people assume that success requires more talent, more intelligence, more opportunity, or more external resources. But people rarely fail because they lack those things. People fail because they cannot consistently manage the energy required to sustain the life they want. They wake up drained, go through the day in survival mode, and allow stress, insecurity, and distraction to override their potential. Their energy is scattered, reactive, and unprotected. They carry emotional weight into spaces where clarity, courage, and conviction are required. And when they approach life with low energy, they receive low results. Then they label life as unfair, when the truth is that their energy was mismanaged.

## 20 Watt: When Life Drains Your Energy

I once worked with a man whose life showed me what drained energy truly looks like. We called him "20 Watt." If you have ever seen a lightbulb that flickers but never fully turns on, that was him. His energy was always low, always dim, always depleted. After spending time with him, I finally asked why his energy stayed so consistently low. He did not hesitate to tell me.

He shared the weight he carried every single day. A dysfunctional family. A second job he worked every night after already completing an eight-hour shift. Financial pressure that never seemed to ease. A severely handicapped son who needed constant care. A wife recovering from a devastating skiing accident. A mountain of responsibilities, a mountain of bills, and a mountain of exhaustion.

He told me he used to love rock climbing, that it was the one thing that made him feel alive, but he had not gone in almost seven years. Life had taken away the time, the freedom, the energy, and the emotional capacity he once had. He felt buried under everything life had thrown at him. He felt trapped. He felt forgotten. He felt like there was no light at the end of the tunnel because he could no longer see one.

His energy was not low because he lacked desire. His energy was low because life had taken far more from him than he had the strength to replenish. He was doing the best he could with the little he had left.

I encouraged him and shared a few strategies on how to become *B.E.T.T.E.R²*. They were simple steps, small openings, and ways to seek professional support. And when he realized that even with everything stacked against him, better was still possible, something shifted inside him. His energy did not rise all at once, but possibility did. And sometimes possibility is the first spark.

Gradually, small changes became visible. Not in his schedule, not in his circumstances, but in his spirit. Everyday life began to feel a little lighter, a little clearer, a little more manageable. And this is where the truth we discussed earlier reveals itself again: energy is your inner climate. It is your attitude in motion, your discipline expressed, your emotional strength revealed, and your focus applied. When that inner climate begins to warm, even slightly, the entire direction of your life begins to change.

His story was extreme, but the truth behind it is universal, when your energy is drained, even the smallest parts of life feel impossible. And this is where most people misunderstand their struggle. They blame their circumstances, their past, or their luck, when the real issue is something far more subtle and far more common energy mismanagement.

> *Energy mismanagement is one of the*
> *quietest forms of self-sabotage.*

You can have the right vision, the right strategy, the right network, and even the right calling, but if your energy is depleted, nothing grows. Low energy creates delays. Low energy creates doubt. Low energy creates emotional fog, inconsistency, impatience, and excuses. When your energy is low, everything feels heavier: the work feels harder, the goals feel farther, the setbacks feel bigger, and the future feels dimmer. Low energy convinces you that you are stuck when in reality you are simply drained.

Elevated energy creates the opposite effect. When your energy is aligned, everything flows with more clarity and strength. You think better, speak better, lead better, love better, and make decisions with more confidence. You respond with wisdom instead of reacting with emotion. You communicate with power instead of insecurity. You attract better opportunities because your energy signals readiness instead of hesitation. High energy does not mean you never get tired; it means you know how to restore yourself, protect yourself, and remain connected to your purpose even when life grows heavy.

**Energy is not an emotion**

Energy is not simply an emotion. Think of your energy like the thermostat of your life. The thermostat decides the temperature of a home, not the weather outside. No matter how cold or chaotic the environment becomes, the thermostat holds its setting and regulates the atmosphere. In the same way, your energy sets the internal temperature of your life. Circumstances may shift, challenges may arise, and unexpected storms may come, but when you control your energetic "thermostat," you control the environment within you and the environment within you shapes everything around you. Energy is who you choose to be in every moment. It is an internal decision before it becomes an external feeling. You can choose clarity even in confusion, peace in chaos, resilience in pressure, and purpose in uncertainty. Energy is a choice long before it becomes a mood. Once you understand that, you stop letting circumstances decide how you show up. You stop letting other people dictate your direction. You stop living emotionally reactive and start living energetically intentional.

> *When you understand that energy is a choice long before it becomes a mood you stop letting other people dictate your direction. You stop living emotionally reactive and start living energetically intentional.*

Yes, it is true you cannot control everything that happens to you, but you always control the energy you bring to it. That is your power. That is your advantage. That is the birthplace of growth.

Energy is deeper than motivation. Motivation rises and falls, but energy is the lifestyle you create. Motivation depends on emotion; energy depends on discipline. Motivation fades under pressure, energy strengthens under purpose. Energy is built by the habits you keep, the environment you choose, the thoughts you allow, and the presence you bring into every moment. When your energy is trained, you become consistent. You move even when you don't feel like it. You show up even when you're not inspired. You keep going even when the path feels unclear. Your energy becomes the proof of your commitment.

Your energy also communicates long before your words do. Confident energy builds trust. Scattered energy pushes people away. Focused energy creates influence. Insecure energy creates hesitation. Passionate energy inspires. Passive energy confuses. Your energy announces whether you are ready for the next level or still negotiating your worth. Whether you lead a home, a business, a relationship, or simply your own life, your energy sets the emotional tone.

**How Your Environment Shapes Your Energy**

Because environment played a role in the Belief chapter, it's important to address it differently here. Environment influences your belief by shaping what you think is possible. But when it comes to energy, environment influences how you feel. Some environments drain energy without ever touching your belief. You can believe deeply in yourself and still feel exhausted by tension, noise, conflict, or emotional heaviness. You can believe in your potential but lose momentum because your surroundings pull on your spirit.

Energy requires moment-to-moment protection. It is shaped by the emotional tone of the room, the behavior of the people around you, the level of chaos versus order in your space, and the rhythms you allow into your day. High-energy people design environments that support clarity rather than confusion, peace rather than pressure, and focus rather than distraction. They are not shaping their environment to change their beliefs that work was done in the first pillar. They shape their environment to support the energy they need to carry out the belief. When your environment is aligned with your purpose, your energy rises. When it is chaotic or draining, your energy leaks even if your belief remains strong.

Your energy affects every corner of your life. Your thinking, your communication, your actions, your responses, your leadership, your relationships, and your spiritual growth. The quality of your energy becomes the quality of your life. When your energy rises, everything connected to you rises as well: your clarity, confidence, creativity, resilience, presence, and results.

Energy is the foundation upon which everything in your life is built. If the foundation is weak, the structure collapses. If the foundation is unstable, the vision suffers. If the foundation is neglected, the dream never grows. You cannot create a powerful life with weak energy. You must cultivate an energy rooted in purpose, strengthened by discipline, aligned with your values, and protected with intention.

Energy is not something you wait for. It is something you build, something you practice, and something you choose. Because in the end, the energy you bring becomes the energy you embody and the energy you embody becomes the life you live. Energy is the Second Pillar to Becoming *B.E.T.T.E.R².* because without mastering your energy, nothing you build can reach its highest version. But once your energy is elevated, you become unstoppable.

**How to Rise From Low Energy to High Energy**

Understanding energy is powerful, but learning how to elevate it is transformational. High energy does not appear overnight, nor does it arrive through luck or inspiration. High energy is built intentionally, consistently, and consciously. It begins with awareness. You cannot rise until you recognize what is holding you down. When you feel drained, unfocused, overwhelmed, or uninspired, it is not a sign of weakness, it is your spirit signaling misalignment. Low energy is not the problem, it is the messenger.

People rise from low energy to high energy by first becoming honest about what is weakening them. Sometimes it is mental overload. Sometimes it is emotional heaviness that has never been addressed. Sometimes it is chronic exhaustion disguised as discouragement. Sometimes it is an unhealthy environment, inconsistent habits, or a life lived without clear purpose. Once you become aware of what drains you, you begin the gradual, intentional work of removing it. You protect your mind from noise, your spirit from conflict, and your time from distraction. As you remove what weakens you, your energy begins to rise because clarity creates space.

The next rise comes from reconnecting to your purpose. Nothing lifts the human spirit faster than direction. When you remember what you are building and why it matters, your confidence returns, your focus sharpens, and your emotional strength awakens. Purpose creates clarity, and clarity creates energy. Most people feel drained not because they are incapable, but because they are disconnected from meaning. When your life gains direction, your energy gains momentum.

Your physical habits play a critical role in your energy as well. A tired body creates a tired mind. You cannot expect high energy from a body that is sleep-deprived, undernourished, dehydrated, or constantly overstimulated. When you strengthen your body, you strengthen your energy. Movement increases clarity. Rest increases resilience. Nutrition increases focus. Hydration improves mood. Physical discipline fuels emotional discipline because the body and mind rise together.

Releasing emotional weight is another essential step. People carry stress, resentment, disappointment, guilt, and unprocessed fear without realizing how much these emotions drain the spirit. You cannot feel light while holding what is heavy. High energy requires internal space. When you forgive, release, and let go, you clear room for strength, clarity, and momentum to return. Emotional release creates energetic freedom.

Your environment must also evolve as your energy rises. Your surroundings shape your spirit differently than they shape your belief. Clutter drains focus; chaos drains confidence; negativity drains motivation. High-energy people create environments that reflect peace, order, inspiration, and growth. They're mindful of the conversations they entertain, the people who have access to their spirit, and the spaces they choose to occupy. When your environment supports your emotional well-being, your energy grows effortlessly.

Mental discipline is where the rise becomes permanent. High energy requires a mind trained to refocus, reframe, and redirect itself. You must control your thoughts rather than allowing your thoughts to control you. People with high energy practice gratitude, interrupt negative spirals, focus on solutions, and protect their attention. A mind trained to stay steady produces a life that moves forward.

People rise into high energy through renewal. You must invest in the practices that bring your spirit alive whether it's prayer, silence, nature, music, creativity, reading, journaling, or meaningful connection. Renewal is not a luxury; it is a requirement. You cannot fill your life with strength if your spirit is empty. Renewal restores not only your energy, but your identity.

The shift from low energy to high energy is ultimately a decision backed by lifestyle. A person decides they will no longer live drained, overwhelmed, or disconnected. They choose peace, purpose, clarity, discipline, and alignment. They choose the habits, environments, and mindsets that match their destiny. And when they make that choice consistently, their energy rises slowly, steadily, and eventually permanently.

You do not wait for high energy.
You build it.
You choose it.
You live it.

And once your energy rises, everything in your life rises with it. Your clarity strengthens. Your confidence grows. Your discipline sharpens. Your presence deepens. Your relationships evolve. Your purpose expands. Energy elevates every part of who you are becoming.But knowing the power of energy is only the beginning. Transformation requires practice. Your energy rises through daily decisions, intentional habits, and consistent alignment with the future you want to create. The following steps will help you not only understand energy but live it.

## THE ENERGY PRACTICE (Action Steps)

Energy rises through intention, discipline, and alignment. These steps will help you begin elevating your energy immediately and consistently.

### 1. Identify One Energy Drain and Remove It

Write down one thing that has been draining your energy: a habit, a thought, a person, or an environment. Release it or reduce its access to you today. Eliminating one drain creates room for renewal.

### 2. Replace One Low-Energy Habit with a High-Energy Choice

Choose one action you normally take when you feel tired, overwhelmed, or reactive. Replace it with a healthier alternative movement, silence, breath, prayer, or gratitude. Substitution is the fuel of energetic transformation.

### 3. Create a Daily Energy Intention

Write a one-sentence intention for how you want to show up today. Say it every morning before starting your day. Your energy follows the direction you set for it.

## 4. Perform a Three-Minute Reset

Pause at least once today for three minutes of deep, intentional breathing or quiet reflection. Resetting your system increases clarity and emotional stability. A calm mind elevates energetic strength.

## 5. Restore Your Body With One Act of Care

Choose one physical action that refuels you: hydration, stretching, a short walk, rest, or healthier nourishment. The body is the engine of energy, treat it like one.

## 6. Protect Your Peace From One Distraction

Identify one distraction that steals your focus or drains your emotions. Turn it off, silence it, or distance yourself from it. Peace is the container where energy grows.

## 7. Do One Action That Raises Your Vibration

Choose one thing that makes you feel alive: music, prayer, movement, journaling, fresh air, sunlight, gratitude, or meaningful connection. Do it with intention. Energy expands when you choose joy on purpose.

*"Talent is not discovered in you, it is developed by you through discipline, repetition, and belief."* — *Sylvester Mayo*

# CHAPTER THREE

# TALENT

## The Third Pillar of Personal Reinvention

*"Talent is not what you are born with,*
*it is what you build when no one is*
*watching."* — *Sylvester Mayo*

Talent is one of the most misunderstood forces of human growth. People think talent is a gift bestowed at birth, a natural advantage that some have and others don't. But real talent has very little to do with what you start with. Real talent is built. Developed. Cultivated. Refined. Strengthened. It is the result of deliberate practice, disciplined repetition, intentional learning, and the humility to grow beyond where you are.

Belief determines what is possible. Energy determines how you show up. But talent determines what you can sustain, deliver, and mastery.

Talent is the difference between hoping and executing. Between potential and performance. Between intention and impact. Where Belief gives you vision and Energy gives you movement, Talent gives you mastery, the ability to do the work at a level that commands respect, opens doors, and creates opportunity that lasts.

Talent is not the presence of natural ability, it is the absence of excuses. People do not fail because they lack talent. They fail because they never trained, never practiced deeply enough, never allowed correction to sharpen them, never allowed discipline to transform them, and never allowed consistency to elevate them.

You can inherit a gift, but you must build talent. You can be born with potential, but you must create competency. You can be given an opportunity, but you must earn mastery. Talent is the commitment to excellence even when no one is clapping. Talent is the willingness to practice until you become undeniable. Talent is skill multiplied by effort, refined through pressure, and rewarded through perseverance.

Two people can start in the same place, same job, same opportunity, same time, same tools but one will rise higher, faster, and farther because they developed their talent while the other relied on natural ability. Natural ability may get you noticed, but trained talent gets you remembered.

Talent is also more than skill. It is purpose expressed through excellence. It is a calling expressed through discipline. It is leadership expressed through mastery. Because when you build your talent, you do not just improve your performance you elevate your identity. You raise your standards. You strengthen your confidence. You sharpen your instincts. You gain the ability to adapt, create, innovate, and excel regardless of the circumstances around you. You become a person people trust, follow, depend on, and invest in. Because talent is credibility. Talent is consistency. Talent is proof.

Greatness is not discovered, it is developed through daily practice. Most people never reach mastery because they quit in the stage where talent is formed: the stage of repetition, the stage of correction, the stage of obscurity, the stage where you practice without recognition, applause, or reward. Mastery is invisible for a long time. It grows in silence. It strengthens in private. It becomes undeniable only after years of refinement.

Every master was once a beginner drowning in mistakes. Every expert was once a student fumbling through basics. Every high performer was once insecure, unpolished, and uncertain.

But the difference between those who rise and those who remain average is simple: the willingness to keep training long after others become comfortable.

Talent grows in the moments no one sees early mornings, late nights, quiet decisions, daily improvements, small corrections, intentional repetitions, the unglamorous work that most people avoid. Because talent is not what you do occasionally; talent is who you become consistently.

## THE TRUTH ABOUT HIDDEN TALENT

"A wise man once told me, you do not have to be great to start, but you do have to start to be great." I carried that line with me for many years. It is a subtle truth with a powerful message: talent is not something you are simply born with, it is something you recognize, develop, and grow into. Most people misunderstand talent. They assume it begins fully formed, but real talent begins the moment you decide to start.

I once met a young woman who insisted she had no talent. She said she could not sing. Believed she was not pretty enough. Questioned her intelligence. And in every room she entered, she felt painfully average. Shy, soft-spoken, and visibly uncomfortable in her own presence, she often hid behind people and conversations, doing anything she could to remain unseen. For years, she compared her life to the strengths of others, never realizing one simple truth: every person she admired once had to start before they became great.

As we talked, doubt echoed through every sentence she spoke. So I asked about the things that made her feel alive, the moments that energized her, the tasks that felt natural, the abilities she performed without effort. I was not coaching her; I was guiding her back to the parts of herself she had quietly abandoned. And in that moment, without fully knowing it, she took her first small step toward becoming *B.E.T.T.E.R²*.

But the more she shared, the more undeniable it became: this woman had a remarkable gift for cooking. Not just "good food" or something that tasted nice. I mean food that made people stop mid-bite. Food that made people close their eyes. Food that made people feel loved, comforted, understood, and seen. She had a gift that translated emotion into flavor, warmth, love, soul, and connection expressed through her hands, heart, and intuition. Yet she never considered cooking a talent. And that is where most people misunderstand their gift. People assume talent must be glamorous, public, loud, dramatic, or validated by the world, but talent rarely begins that way. Talent is often quiet, subtle, soft, deep, and personal. It hides in what you do naturally, in what you enjoy without effort, in what others feel but you overlook, and in the beauty you assume is ordinary.

Most people do not pursue their gift because they do not think highly enough of themselves. They cannot imagine earning a living from something that feels so natural. They convince themselves it "does not count" because it does not resemble someone else's version of talent. But talent does not need permission to be valuable, it needs recognition, development, and belief. She never recognized her gift because it was not glamorous, but what she carried was leadership, because food brought people together. It was emotional intelligence, because she sensed what people needed. It was empathy, because she cooked with compassion. It was influence, because her food shifted atmospheres. It was excellence, because she elevated whatever she touched. And it was rare, beautiful, and extraordinary.

People often overlook their greatest talent because it feels too natural to them, but what is natural to you may be miraculous to someone else. I could see her doubt and her uncertainty. She genuinely believed she had nothing special. So I shared the *B.E.T.T.E.R².* principles with her, the same ones you are learning in this book. We talked about belief. We talked about energy. We talked about talent. We talked about time. We talked about enlisting support. We talked about reading, learning, and growing. She listened quietly, still shy, still unsure, still hiding but something inside her shifted. A spark formed. And sometimes a spark is enough.

Years later, she reached out to me. She told me she began cooking for friends, then neighbors, then small events. She studied recipes, read books, learned techniques, and practiced intentionally. She asked for feedback. She refined her craft. She built confidence through consistency. Pop-ups sold out. Private dinners booked months in advance. A small kitchen became a business. A business became a restaurant. A restaurant became a chain. Today, she is a multi-millionaire restaurateur with lines out the door every single day.

But here is what matters most, it was never about the money. The money was the result, not the reward. The real reward was discovering her gift, honoring her passion, disciplining her craft, and realizing the talent she had carried inside her the entire time. She became better.

Her story is not about food. Her story is about awakening. Her story is about identity. Her story is about recognizing the greatness within you before the world sees it. Because when you discover your gift, hone it with discipline, and finally realize the talent within you, your entire life begins to rise.

## The Talent Within You

Talent is not something you sit around waiting to discover. Talent is something you activate, something you cultivate, something you grow into with intention and responsibility. It begins the moment you decide to stop underestimating yourself and start to strengthen the moment you stop comparing your abilities to the abilities of others. Every person carries a hidden brilliance sometimes buried under fear, sometimes hidden beneath insecurity, sometimes silenced because life convinced them they were average or replaceable. But there is nothing average about the gift placed inside you. There is nothing ordinary about the way you think, create, connect, or contribute. There is a reason certain tasks feel natural to you, why some ideas pull at your spirit, and why certain activities make you come alive. Your talent is always speaking; most people simply stop listening.

Talent cannot evolve in hesitation, fear, or environments filled with doubt and procrastination. If you want to become *B.E.T.T.E.R².*, you must be willing to do the work of mastery, the work most people avoid. This is the unglamorous work, the repetitive work, the quiet work done long before anyone claps for you. It is the early-morning practice, the late-night refinement, the daily corrections, and the moments of private discipline that eventually lead to public excellence. You do not need perfect conditions, ideal timing, or universal approval to strengthen your talent. You do not need permission. What you need is a simple but life-altering decision: the decision to start. Because once you start, consistency begins to build its own momentum. Confidence grows. Competency expands. And slowly, the talent you once doubted becomes the talent everyone else can clearly see.

As you move forward, ask yourself: What ability have I ignored? What skill have I dismissed? What strength have I minimized? What passion have I allowed life to bury? Your talent is not waiting for validation; it is waiting for action. The greatest version of you is not hiding; it is simply undeveloped. But the moment you commit to refining your gift with discipline, humility, passion, and perseverance, your entire life begins to rise. Talent is the Third Pillar to Becoming *B.E.T.T.E.R².* because talent is where belief becomes visible and where energy becomes productive. Talent is where potential turns into performance and where intention transforms into impact. You are not behind. You are not lacking. You are not finished. You are becoming. And now is the time to master what is already yours.

**THE TALENT PRACTICE (Action Steps)**

**How to Build, Strengthen, and Master Your Gift**

Talent grows through repetition, discipline, and intentional development. These steps will help you begin strengthening your talent immediately and consistently.

**1. Identify One Natural Ability You Have Ignored**

Take a moment to reflect on something that comes naturally to you, something others have complimented, relied on, or noticed, even if you dismissed it. Write it down. Name it clearly. Talent begins with awareness, and the moment you acknowledge a natural ability, you give yourself permission to develop it.

**2. Choose One Skill to Practice With Intention**

Pick a single skill connected to your talent and commit to practicing it deliberately this week. Not casually. Not when convenient. Intentionally. Set aside a short, focused block of time each day to refine that skill. Progress will feel small at first, but consistency builds competence, and competence builds confidence.

### 3. Study One Person Who Has Mastered What You Want to Learn

Choose someone whose excellence inspires you and study their process, not their results. Read interviews, watch videos, observe their discipline, and take notes on what you can apply. Mastery leaves clues, and learning from someone ahead of you accelerates your development.

### 4. Ask for One Piece of Honest Feedback

Growth requires refinement, and refinement requires feedback. Ask someone you trust to give you one clear, constructive insight about your talent. Listen with openness, not defensiveness. Feedback is not criticism, feedback is guidance. One honest observation can save you years of guessing.

### 5. Create a Consistency Ritual

Talent strengthens when it becomes part of your lifestyle. Create a small ritual that keeps your talent in motion for ten minutes of practice, reading one page, reviewing notes, or studying one new technique. The ritual does not need to be long, only consistent. What you do daily becomes who you become permanently.

## 6. Remove One Excuse That Has Been Limiting Your Growth

Every person has at least one excuse that quietly weakens their potential: "I do not have enough time," "I am not good enough yet," or "I do not know where to start." Identify the excuse that shows up most often in your mind and replace it with a new belief and a new action. Excuses drain talent; responsibility develops it.

## 7. Do One Bold Act That Honors Your Gift

Before this week ends, take one bold step that stretches you: share your work, volunteer your talent, apply for an opportunity, take a class, showcase your ability, or create something new. Boldness awakens talent. When you honor your gift publicly or privately, your talent begins to rise.

*"Time does not multiply; purpose does. When you align your hours with your calling, your life accelerates."* — *Sylvester Mayo*

## CHAPTER FOUR

# TIME

### The Fourth Pillar of Personal Reinvention

*"Time is the only resource you are guaranteed
but never promised more of. Master it, or
life will master you."* — Sylvester Mayo

As an avid reader and lifelong student of personal growth, I have spent years studying self-help, personal development, and the psychology of human behavior. Yet even with all that knowledge, I often found myself facing a familiar struggle: trying to find enough time. My work requires constant travel, long hours, and unpredictable demands. I am away from home more than I prefer, and because of that, the things I enjoy or desire to do often get pushed aside. Time always seemed to move faster than I could keep up with, and no matter how much I planned or organized, it never felt like enough.

On a recent business trip to Dubai, I opened a small but powerful book called *Rhythms of Life* by William E. Bailey. Bailey was an entrepreneur, a speaker, the founder of several successful companies, and a pioneer in the world of personal development. He was also a close friend and early influence on Jim Rohn, one of the greatest motivational teachers of our era. What Bailey wrote in that book shifted my understanding of time more than anything I had ever studied.

In one chapter, Bailey told the story of a man who constantly prayed the same request: "God, give me more time." Every day, the man begged for more hours, believing that the only thing standing between him and a better life was a longer day. As I read his desperation, I saw myself in him. I saw the countless moments I whispered that same thought, believing that if my day just had a little more room, I could finally catch up, finally rest, finally accomplish everything pulling at my mind and heart.

But then came God's response, simple, direct, and transformational.

**"I cannot give you more time. Give Me more of you."**

Those words struck me with a force I cannot describe. They dismantled every excuse I had ever made about time. They revealed a truth I had avoided for years. We do not receive more hours in the day. Time does not increase. Time does not bend to our desires or stretch to accommodate our dreams. Time is fixed. Time is limited. Time is non-negotiable. But what can expand, what must expand, is us.

We do not need more time, we need more intention. We do not need additional hours; we need more focus. We do not need the day to stretch; we need our discipline to stretch. Time will not change for us, but we can change how we show up in the time we are given.

Sitting on that plane, looking out over the clouds on the way to Dubai, I realized something that shifted the way I live my life: I did not have a time problem, I had a stewardship problem. I was asking God for more hours when I was not even fully using the hours I already had. Time was not the issue. My management of time was the issue. My presence within the time I had was the issue. My discipline, focus, and priorities were the issue.

From that moment on, I stopped asking for "more time" and started asking myself a different question: How can I give more of myself to the same twenty-four hours everyone else has? That single question changed everything. It made time sacred. It made time valuable. It made time intentional. It made time personal. It became clear that time was never my enemy. Time was my teacher showing me what mattered, exposing what I neglected, and revealing who I needed to become.

And now, as you enter the Fourth Pillar of Becoming *B.E.T.T.E.R²*., you are about to experience that same shift. Because once you understand the truth about time, you stop living rushed, overwhelmed, and reactive. You start living purposefully, disciplined, and aligned. Time has never been the barrier to your next level. Time has always been the key.

## The Illusion of Not Enough Time, Why Most People Stay Stuck

Most people believe they are overwhelmed because they do not have enough time. They say it often and with conviction: "I would change my life if I had more time." "I would start the business if I had more time." "I would work on my goals, exercise, write, study, or improve if only I had more time." It sounds true, it feels true, and it is one of the most common explanations people use to justify their frustration or lack of progress.

But the truth is far more uncomfortable: People do not lack time. People lack clarity, structure, discipline, and focus.

The feeling of "not enough time" is rarely about the clock. It is about how the mind interacts with time. When your mind is scattered, your time becomes scattered. When your priorities are unclear, your schedule becomes cluttered. When your emotional energy is low, even simple tasks feel overwhelming. What most people experience is not a shortage of hours, it is a shortage of intentionality.

The illusion of "not enough time" is created by three major forces:

## 1. The Overwhelm of Unmade Decisions

Every unmade decision takes up space in your mind. When your brain holds too many open loops, tasks you have not clarified, moments you have not organized, responsibilities you have not mapped out it creates cognitive overwhelm.

Overwhelm makes time feel shorter, even though the hours have not changed.

*A vague life is an overwhelming life. A clear life is an empowered one.*

## 2. The Addiction to Distraction

Distraction is the modern thief of potential. Phones, social media, endless scrolling, constant notifications, emotional noise, and digital interruptions steal minutes, then hours, then days without you realizing it. Distractions train your brain for short bursts of attention, making it difficult to engage deeply with anything meaningful.

*You cannot build a powerful life on a distracted mind.*

## 3. The Mismanagement of Emotional Energy

We touched on this in the Energy pillar: when your energy is low, everything feels harder. And when everything feels harder, you lose time. A drained mind moves slowly. A stressed mind makes poor decisions. A tired spirit wastes precious moments trying to gather strength that should have been protected.

**Time feels shorter when your energy is scattered.**

Time itself is not the issue. The issue is what fills your mind and consumes your capacity. Think about how different your day feels when you are inspired versus when you are discouraged. When you are motivated versus when you are apathetic. When you are disciplined versus when you are unfocused. Time does not speed up or slow down but your relationship with time does. Most people are not short on time; they are short on alignment. They give their best hours to the least important tasks. They give their attention to noise instead of purpose. They give their energy to urgency instead of priority. They live in reaction instead of intention. When your time is unprotected, your life becomes unfulfilled. The illusion of "not enough time" keeps people trapped because it gives them a reason not to change. It allows them to blame the day instead of examining their decisions. But as long as time is the enemy, you never take responsibility for how you use it. And without responsibility, mastery is impossible.

The moment you stop saying, "I do not have enough time," and start asking, "How am I using the time I already have?" everything shifts. You move from victim to steward. From overwhelmed to organized. From reactive to intentional.

From rushed to purposeful. You start influencing your hours instead of letting your hours control you.

And that is the beginning of time mastery: Not more hours. More ownership.

## The Time Is a Mirror: What Your Schedule Says About Your Destiny

Your schedule is one of the most honest reflections of your life. It reveals what you value, what you fear, what you avoid, what you pursue, and what you are becoming. People often speak about their dreams, passions, and goals with conviction, but their schedule quietly tells a very different story. You can declare that you want to be financially free, emotionally stronger, spiritually grounded, physically healthier, or more successful, but if your time does not align with those desires, the gap between your vision and your reality will only widen.

Most people misunderstand time because they treat their schedule like a suggestion instead of a strategy. A schedule is not merely a list of appointments or responsibilities it is the architecture of your future. Every decision you make about how to spend your hours is a vote for the kind of life you will eventually live. Time either builds your destiny or delays it, depending on how deliberately you use it.

If you want to know where your life is headed, examine three things:your habits, your commitments, and your calendar. They will always tell the truth.

Many people say they want transformation, but their time shows hesitation. They say they want growth, but their hours reveal procrastination. They say they want success, but their daily decisions reveal distraction and inconsistency. Your destiny is not created in your intentions, it is created in your intervals, the small pockets of time where you choose whether to invest in your future or indulge in your comfort.

Your schedule reveals patterns that speak louder than any motivational declaration. It shows whether you prioritize your purpose or your problems. It shows whether you protect your potential or surrender it to distractions. It shows whether you live by design or by default. It is impossible to hide from time because time records everything: every choice, every delay, every habit, and every excuse. Your future is written in how you spend the minutes no one sees.

This is why people who master their destiny master their schedule first. They understand that time is not emotional, it is mathematical. The future does not respond to feelings, it responds to patterns. The people who rise are not always the most gifted, but they are the ones who learn to discipline their time. They build routines that support their purpose. They create structures that eliminate chaos. They develop habits that reinforce their identity. They design days that support their future instead of repeating their past.

If your schedule is filled with distractions, your destiny will drift. If your schedule is filled with excuses, your destiny will shrink. If your schedule is filled with intentionality, your destiny will expand. Time reveals what you truly believe about yourself. If you believe you are capable, you invest time in growth. If you believe you are unworthy, you waste time avoiding your potential. If you believe you are called to greatness, your time reflects your calling.

The most successful, fulfilled, and disciplined people are not lucky, they are intentional. They treat their time with the same seriousness as others treat their money. They guard their mornings, protect their evenings, and use their hours with purpose. They know they cannot control everything that happens in life, but they refuse to let their schedule become a reflection of chaos. They make time their ally, not their enemy. Your schedule is a mirror. And if you have the courage to look into it without excuses, you will see the truth that can change your life. Because the moment you align your time with your destiny is the moment your destiny becomes inevitable.

There comes a point in every person's life where they must face a difficult truth, you cannot get to the next level if everything in your life still has equal importance. Not everything deserves your time. Not every task deserves your energy. Not every demand deserves your attention. The people who live effective, meaningful, destiny-driven lives are not the people who do the most. They are the people who prioritize the best. They understand that when everything matters, nothing truly moves forward. Success requires separation. Growth requires discernment. Purpose requires clarity. You must learn to separate the urgent from the important, the loud from the meaningful, and the temporary from the transformational.

Time does not expand just because your dreams do. You do not get extra hours simply because your goals become bigger. Instead, you become a better steward of the hours you already have. Priority is the discipline of aligning your time with your destiny. It requires asking hard questions: *Does this move me forward? Does this strengthen the future I am building? Does this reflect the life I say I want?* When the answer is no, the decision is simple: you release it. When the answer is yes, you give it focus, excellence, and consistency.

One of the most powerful shifts you can make in life is deciding that your time will no longer be controlled by pressure, reaction, or obligation. You choose what stays. You choose what goes. You choose what receives your effort, what receives your energy, and what receives your presence. Priority is not about doing less; it is about increasing the value of the time you invest. It is about placing your hours where your future lives. It is about removing distractions so your purpose can finally breathe.

The greatest breakthroughs in life do not happen when people find more time. They happen when people refuse to waste the time they already have. They stop apologizing for protecting their focus. They stop feeling guilty for saying no. They stop allowing other people's chaos to steal their clarity. They honor the life they are building by honoring the time required to build it. And as their priorities sharpen, their results accelerate. Their confidence grows. Their discipline strengthens. Their life transforms because their time finally matches their vision.

This is the power of priority: when you choose what matters most, your time multiplies, your purpose expands, and your destiny unfolds with greater precision and greater peace. Priority is not just a skill, it is a spiritual responsibility. It is the difference between living accidentally and living intentionally. It is the difference between being busy and being effective. It is the difference between wasting years and building a legacy. Because the moment you choose priority, you choose the life you were truly meant to live.

## THE TIME PRACTICE (Action Steps)

Time only grows in value when you grow in discipline. These steps will help you align your time with your purpose and elevate how you live each day.

### 1. Claim Your 24 Hours With Intention

Before the world asks anything of you, decide who you will be today. Write a one-sentence intention each morning: *"Today, I will…"* This transforms your day from reactive to purposeful. When you claim your intention, you take ownership of your time instead of letting time take ownership of you.

### 2. Identify One Time Leak and Close It

Every life has silent thieves, habits, distractions, or patterns that drain hours without you noticing. Pick one. Just one. Then remove it or reduce it significantly for the next seven days. You will be shocked at how much time returns to you when leakage is eliminated.

### 3. Block Your Non-Negotiables

Purpose is protected by boundaries. Choose your non-negotiables, reading, prayer, working out, planning, rest and put them on your schedule first. Not after work. Not "if time allows." Your calendar becomes powerful when it reflects your priorities instead of your problems.

### 4. Create a "Purpose Hour"

Set aside one uninterrupted hour each day to pour into the future you're building. No phone. No notifications. No multitasking. Just one focused hour devoted to your growth, dreams, and long-term goals. Most people do not lack time, they lack focused time. One purpose hour a day changes everything.

### 5. Perform a Daily Time Audit

At the end of the day, review how you used your time. Not with judgment through observation. Where did you grow? Where did you drift? Where did you waste energy? This simple five-minute audit strengthens awareness, and awareness strengthens discipline.

## 6. Say "No" to One Thing This Week

Time expands when you learn how to protect it. Identify one commitment, invitation, task, or expectation that drains you or misaligns you. Say no politely, clearly, and confidently. Every "no" creates room for the "yes" your future needs.

## 7. Do One Thing Your Future Self Will Thank You For

Each day, choose one action, just one that moves you closer to the life you are building. Send the email. Make the call. Read the chapter. Study the skill. Clean the space. Prepare the plan. Your future expands when your present self acts with intention.

*"You rise higher when you stop climbing alone; no destiny is reached without a village."* — *Sylvester Mayo*

# CHAPTER FIVE

# ENLIST SUPPORT

**The Fifth Pillar of Personal Reinvention**

*"You can do a lot alone, but you
will never reach your highest level
by yourself."* — *Sylvester Mayo*

Support is not a luxury. Support is a strategy. And for most people, it is the strategy they resist the longest. We live in a culture that glorifies independence, celebrates grinding alone, and praises the idea of being "self-made." Yet anyone who has ever reached greatness athletes, entrepreneurs, leaders, scholars, creators, parents, visionaries knows the truth: nobody becomes their best self by themselves. There is always a team, a mentor, a guide, a friend, a partner, or a community that helped shape the journey.

There's a reason people have used the proverb over the years "It takes a village to raise a child." It isn't just about parenting it's about becoming. A child grows through the influence, wisdom, and presence of many different people. Every teacher shapes a mindset. Every mentor sharpens a skill. Every family member adds a layer of love, protection, or discipline. A child becomes stronger because a village surrounds them. And the same truth applies to adults. If it takes a village to raise a child, it takes a *community* to raise a dream. It takes support to raise a vision. It takes guidance to raise a new version of yourself. No great life is ever built alone. Greatness may look individual from the outside, but behind the scenes there is always a village, a circle, a team, a tribe holding the person up, speaking into them, challenging them, supporting them, and lifting them toward their next level.

Here is what I want you to know: belief gives you vision. Energy gives you movement. Talent gives you mastery. Time gives you structure. But support gives you acceleration. Support expands your capacity. Support strengthens your resilience. Support challenges your blind spots. Support protects your progress. Support multiplies your impact. People do not fail because they lack ability; people fail because they insist on carrying everything alone. And when you carry everything alone, the weight eventually breaks what your potential was trying to build.

Most people resist support for one of three reasons: pride, pain, or pattern. Pride says, "I don't need anyone." Pain says, "I don't trust anyone." Pattern says, "I've always done it alone." But growth requires a new choice, and becoming *B.E.T.T.E.R²*. requires a new community.

> *The truth is, support only becomes real the moment you allow someone who has traveled farther than you to guide you through a road you've never driven before.*

When I was teaching my oldest son to drive, we practiced for months on wide roads, city streets, mall parking lots and familiar routes where the environment felt safe. Then one evening, just after dark, I took him far into the countryside. No streetlights. No markings. Nothing but a narrow road stretching into the unknown. I pulled over and told him, "I want you to drive us home."

He looked around and immediately panicked. "Shouldn't we turn around and go back the way we came?" he asked. I shook my head. "No. This road is one big circle. If you stay on it long enough, it will bring you right back to the same highway we turned off." He gripped the steering wheel. "Dad, I don't think I can do it. I can't even tell where the road is going." I could hear the fear in his voice. The uncertainty. The doubt. So I told him, "Don't worry. Just listen to me. Slow down when I say slow down. Speed up when I say speed up. Prepare to stop when I tell you to stop. If you can follow my voice, we'll get home safely."

And he did. Every turn. Every dip. Every blind curve. He drove forward through the dark, guided only by the voice of someone who had already traveled that road many times before. When we finally pulled into the driveway, he turned to me and asked, "Dad how did you know all that? All those turns, all those details how?"

I smiled and said, "Because I grew up on that road. I have lived on it most of my life."

That is what mentors do. They see the potholes you do not see. They know the sharp curves before you reach them. They warn you about the stop signs hidden in the dark. They guide you through roads that feel unfamiliar because they have already lived through them.

Support works the same way someone who has already lived through what you are trying to navigate can help you avoid the unseen dangers, the sharp turns, and the hidden obstacles that you cannot yet recognize.

You cannot rise to your next level while holding onto the same isolated habits. The greatest transformations in life happen through connection divine connection, strategic connection, emotional connection, and purposeful connection. Every season of growth demands someone who speaks life into you, someone who sharpens you, someone who supports you, and someone who holds you accountable to who you said you want to become.

Support is not weakness; it is wisdom. Support is not dependency; it is development. Support is not surrender; it is strength. You become stronger when you are supported. You become wiser when you are advised. You become better when you are connected. The Fifth Pillar is the reminder that your destiny is too big for you to walk into it alone, and that every future you desire will require the right people, the right guidance, and the right voices around you.

## The Four Forms of Support You Must Enlist

Once you understand that support is not optional but essential, the next step is learning how to choose the right kind of support. Not every voice deserves access to your future, and not every person belongs in the next chapter of your life. Becoming *B.E.T.T.E.R².* requires intentional relationships with people who add strength to your journey rather than weight to your spirit. Growth is never random; it is shaped by the quality of the people you allow near your vision. And if you want your life to accelerate, you must enlist four specific forms of support: Mentors, Models, Mirrors, and Multipliers.

**Mentors** are the individuals who know the road ahead. They have walked the path you are now walking, experienced the failures you have yet to face, and gained the wisdom you cannot acquire alone. A mentor shortens your learning curve, protects you from unnecessary mistakes, and expands your vision by showing you what is possible beyond your current level of understanding. They are not there to live your life for you, but to strengthen the wisdom within you.

**Models** create clarity through demonstration. Their life becomes a blueprint you can study and learn from. A model may never mentor you directly, but their habits, discipline, character, and results provide insight into what it takes to rise. Models give your dreams shape by showing you what they look like in reality. They remind you that greatness is not mysterious; it is structured, built, and maintained through consistent standards.

**Mirrors** are the people who tell you the truth. They reflect back who you are—not the image you present, but the reality of your patterns, excuses, and blind spots. Real growth is impossible without honest feedback, and mirrors offer clarity where your perspective is limited. They challenge you when you shrink. They remind you when you drift. They hold you accountable to the person you committed to becoming. Without mirrors, growth becomes accidental. With mirrors, growth becomes intentional.

**Multipliers** elevate your spirit simply through their presence. These are the people who make you better by being around them. They sharpen your focus, heighten your standards, increase your confidence, and bring out the version of you that you often forget is there. Multipliers do not compete with you, they collaborate with you. They do not drain you, they energize you. They see your potential clearly, even when you momentarily lose sight of it yourself.

When you enlist these four forms of support, your entire life transforms. Your belief strengthens because you have mentors guiding your path. Your vision sharpens because you have models revealing what is possible. Your character grows because mirrors keep you aligned with your truth. Your confidence rises because multipliers elevate how you see yourself.

Support is not an accident. Support is not coincidence. Support is not something you "hope" for. Support is the strategy that turns possibility into progress.

## How to Find the Right Support (When You Have No Idea Where to Start)

Most people know they need support. What they do not know is *how to find it.* They do not know where mentors come from, how to attract the right guidance, how to recognize the people assigned to their growth, or how to build relationships with people who are ahead of them. So they struggle alone not because they want to be isolated, but because no one ever taught them how to build a circle that elevates their future.

I have traveled the world speaking, teaching, and sharing the principles you are learning in this book. From large corporate audiences to intimate leadership rooms, from colleges to conferences to community gatherings, people often approach me afterward with the same question: "Can you be my mentor?" They ask with sincerity, hunger, and hope. They want direction. They want clarity. They want guidance. But here is what most people do not understand: mentorship is not requested; mentorship is earned. It is not something you ask for; it is something you attract.

Mentors are drawn to consistency, effort, humility, and hunger, not words alone. The people who come to me after events wanting mentorship often mean well, but many are asking for someone to build their life *for them*, not *with them*. They want the result without the responsibility. They want transformation without discipline. A true mentor cannot carry you; they can only guide someone willing to walk.

Finding a mentor starts with becoming someone who is mentor-able. That means you show initiative without being asked. You take action without needing permission. You are already working before you meet the person you want guidance from. Mentors invest in people who are already investing in themselves. This is not just from a financial perspective. They pour into people who are moving, not waiting. They guide people who are willing to do the work.

If you want a mentor, you do not begin by asking for one, you begin by preparing for one. You rise in your discipline. You sharpen your habits. You show consistency in the areas you claim to care about. When someone sees your effort, they see your potential. And potential attracts support.

But mentors are only one part of your support system. Models, mirrors, and multipliers follow the same principle: *you attract who you become.* If you want high-level relationships, you must elevate the level at which you live. Raise your standards, and your circle will rise to meet them. Discipline draws disciplined people. Excellence draws excellence. Purpose draws purpose. Growth draws growth.

The second key to finding support is positioning yourself where growth-minded people gather. You cannot meet a mentor if you remain hidden. You cannot find models if you stay in rooms where no one is rising. You cannot develop mirrors if you never engage with honest people. You cannot discover multipliers in environments that drain you. Support becomes accessible when you place yourself in environments where your future is respected.

Attend workshops. Join masterminds. Serve at events. Volunteer in spaces that align with your destiny. Reach out to people whose work inspires you. Most importantly do not be afraid. Engage with communities that value growth. Mentors appear when you commit to the process. Models appear when you study those who are ahead of you. Mirrors appear when you build relationships rooted in truth, not convenience. Multipliers appear when you enter rooms that require the next version of you.

And the third key is learning how to ask the right way. Mentorship is not, "Can you guide my life?" Mentorship is, "Here is what I am already doing, can you help me refine it?" Models are not asked to validate you; they are observed so you can grow. Mirrors are not demanded, they are trusted because their honesty earns your respect. Multipliers are not forced, they connect because they recognize alignment in your spirit.

Support finds those who are ready for it. Support remains with those who honor it. Support grows with those who apply it.

Finding the right support does not start with looking outward, it starts with looking inward. When you elevate who you are, you elevate who you attract. When you invest in your growth, you connect with people who grow. When you commit to becoming *B.E.T.T.E.R²*., you naturally align with people who are committed to becoming greater, deeper, stronger, and wiser.

And when you find the right circle, your destiny begins to accelerate in ways you could never achieve alone.

## THE SUPPORT PRACTICE (Action Steps)

Support is not something you wait for. Support is something you build with intention. These steps will help you begin forming the relationships, guidance, and community that will accelerate your path to becoming *B.E.T.T.E.R²*.

### 1. Identify One Area Where You Need Support

Begin by choosing one part of your life where support would create the greatest difference: your career, your habits, your finances, your discipline, your emotional health, or your personal growth. Write it down. Clarity opens the door for the right guidance to appear. When you know exactly where you need help, you become aligned with the people who can help you rise.

### 2. Find One Mentor You Can Learn From Indirectly

You do not need direct access to someone for them to mentor you. Choose one person whose life reflects the results you want. An author, a speaker, a leader, an entrepreneur, a creator and study them intentionally. Read their books. Watch their interviews. Learn their process. Growth begins the moment you become a student of excellence.

## 3. Join One Growth-Minded Environment

Place yourself in a room, community, class, or group filled with people committed to becoming better. Growth happens faster when you are surrounded by people who value discipline, accountability, and direction. Your environment will do half the work for you if you choose it intentionally.

## 4. Identify One Mirror—Someone Who Can Tell You the Truth

Think of a person in your life who is honest, grounded, and trustworthy. Someone who can lovingly point out your blind spots without tearing you down. Invite them into your growth journey. Accountability accelerates transformation, because truth is the doorway through which change enters your life.

## 5. Connect With One Multiplier

A multiplier is someone whose presence lifts your energy, sharpens your perspective, and encourages your potential. Choose one person who embodies the future you want to build and begin nurturing that relationship. Spend more time around the people who expand you and less time around the people who drain you.

## 6. Take One Action That Makes You "Mentor-Ready"

Do something today that demonstrates seriousness about your growth, complete a task you have been avoiding, refine a skill, increase your consistency, or practice discipline in a small but meaningful way. Mentors are drawn to movement. Excellence attracts the eyes of people who can help you rise.

## 7. Serve Before You Seek

Offer value before you request guidance. Support someone else's vision. Help where you can. Contribute to a project, event, or mission that aligns with your purpose. Service opens doors that ambition alone cannot. The more you give, the more you grow and the more support naturally finds its way back to you.

*"Reading expands the mind, sharpens identity, and introduces you to the version of yourself you have not yet met."* — *Sylvester Mayo*

## CHAPTER SIX

# READ

**The Sixth Pillar of Personal Reinvention**

*"Readers don't just turn pages, readers turn destinies." — Sylvester Mayo*

There is a powerful line I once heard that shook me awake: "People read so little they have rickets of the mind." It sounds humorous at first, but the truth hidden inside it is anything but a joke. Rickets is a physical condition caused by a lack of vitamin D, calcium, or sunlight, the essential nutrients the body needs to build strong, healthy bones. When those nutrients are missing, the bones become soft, weak, underdeveloped, and easily damaged. The body collapses under pressure not because it is flawed, but because it was never properly nourished.

The same thing happens to the mind. When a person does not read, does not learn, and does not feed their mind with new ideas, deep wisdom, and meaningful knowledge, their thinking becomes weak in the very same way. Their imagination softens. Their creativity becomes limited. Their perspective narrows. Their ability to solve problems, think critically, and understand themselves and the world becomes fragile. They are not mentally limited because they lack intelligence, but because they lack nourishment. Their mind simply has not been fed.

Just as the body needs nutrients to grow strong, the mind needs books. It needs ideas that stretch it, language that sharpens it, stories that expand it, and wisdom that strengthens it. Without these things, the mind cannot develop the capacity required to handle opportunity, pressure, or purpose. A starving mind will always break under the weight of the life it wants to build. And this is why one truth has echoed through history: all good leaders are good readers. Every great thinker, innovator, builder, creator, entrepreneur, and world-changer sharpened their brilliance through the books they consumed.

***You cannot lead well if you do not
think well, and you cannot think
well if you do not read well.***

That is why this metaphor hits so deeply. It exposes a truth most people miss: a neglected mind quietly sabotages the life trying to grow around it. If you do not feed your mind, your mind becomes sick. If you do not grow your thinking, your life stays small. If you do not read, you repeat the same cycles because you lack the insight required to break them.

Reading is not a hobby. Reading is not something you do "when you have time." Reading is not optional if you intend to evolve. Reading is mental nutrition. It is the foundation that strengthens every other pillar of your life. If Belief sets your vision, Energy fuels your movement, Talent shapes your mastery, Time organizes your structure, and Support accelerates your journey, then Reading is the pillar that fortifies your mind so you can sustain the weight of the life you are building.

People who read expand while others remain limited. They rise while others repeat. They evolve while others stay the same. Reading is one of the few disciplines that turns ordinary thinkers into extraordinary leaders and transforms entire destinies simply through exposure, perspective, and wisdom. It is not just about turning pages, it is about turning into a stronger, wiser, more capable version of yourself.

And if you want to become *B.E.T.T.E.R²*., you must become a lifelong reader.

## THE REALITY ABOUT READING (What Most People Never Admit)

Most people think they read "enough." They believe they learn "enough." They assume their mind is being stretched simply because they consume content online scrolling, watching, swiping, or listening. But the numbers tell a very different story, and the numbers never lie.

The uncomfortable truth is this: the average person barely reads at all. According to multiple national literacy reports, one in three adults did not read a single book last year, not one page from beginning to end. Even more revealing, 54 percent of people who start a nonfiction book never finish it. They begin with good intentions, but distraction wins. Life interrupts. Motivation fades. And the book quietly returns to the shelf while their potential quietly returns to stagnation.

Then there is the gap the one most people never talk about. It is the gap between the average reader and the successful reader. While the average person reads one book or fewer per year, top performers, CEOs, entrepreneurs, thought leaders, and high-level achievers read 60 to 80 books a year. That is not a small difference. That is a canyon. A divide. A separation created not by talent or intelligence, but by habit, discipline, and hunger.

And here is what that gap proves: the mind grows at the level you feed it.

People who do not grow mentally become limited emotionally, creatively, professionally, and spiritually. Their thinking becomes narrow. Their imagination becomes rigid. Their problem-solving weakens. Their worldview shrinks. Their confidence slowly deteriorates because knowledge is the oxygen of personal development when you stop feeding the mind, the mind stops expanding.

When I was young, I used to hear teachers say, *"Reading is fundamental."* Back then, it sounded like a slogan for school. Today, I understand how profound those three words really are. Reading is fundamental not just to education, but to leadership, to growth, to confidence, to perspective, to emotional intelligence, and to the expansion of your entire life. If you do not feed your mind, your thinking becomes fragile. If you do not stretch your mind, your creativity becomes limited. If you do not challenge your mind, your understanding becomes shallow. Reading is not academic; it is foundational.

It is mental nutrition for the spirit, the career, the vision, and the destiny you are building.

Meanwhile, people who read consistently think differently. They communicate with authority. They make decisions with clarity. They approach challenges with creativity. They process emotions more intelligently. They recognize opportunities faster. They build careers, businesses, and lives on a foundation of insight instead of impulse, wisdom instead of luck, perspective instead of panic.

This is why one of the oldest truths remains unshaken: all great leaders are great readers. It does not matter whether they lead a business, a family, a team, a classroom, a community, or a movement leaders read because reading expands them. Reading stretches their vision. Reading sharpens their thinking. Reading gives them access to thousands of minds, mentors, and experiences they would never encounter on their own.

Reading is not a hobby. Reading is a strategy. Reading is leverage. Reading is mental nutrition. And just like the body weakens without vitamins, the mind weakens without wisdom. When people avoid reading, their thoughts develop slowly. Their creativity becomes fragile. Their emotional responses become reactive instead of intentional. Their perspective lacks depth. They end up exactly like we mentioned earlier with "rickets of the mind."

Let the statistics remind you of one thing: If you want an extraordinary life, you cannot think like the majority. And if you cannot think like the majority, you cannot read like the majority. Reading is the difference between living by default and living by design. Between repeating old patterns and writing a new story. Between being shaped by the world and shaping your own world.

In the journey to becoming *B.E.T.T.E.R²*., reading is not optional. It is essential. It is transformative. And it is one of the greatest indicators of where your future is heading.

## HOW READING REWIRES YOUR MIND, YOUR IDENTITY, AND YOUR DESTINY

Reading is not an activity. Reading is an awakening. It is one of the few practices in life that can reach into your mind, rearrange the way you think, introduce you to new possibilities, and elevate you beyond the limits of your environment. When you read, you are not just absorbing words, you are absorbing worlds. You are expanding your imagination, strengthening your reasoning, sharpening your perception, and stretching the borders of what you believe is possible. Reading is one of the few tools on earth that allows you to grow without moving, travel without leaving, and learn without losing time.

Your mind has patterns, grooves, habits, and automatic ways of interpreting the world. These patterns determine how you respond to stress, how you solve problems, how you see opportunity, and how you understand yourself. Most of these patterns were formed unintentionally through childhood, environment, culture, trauma, repetition, and survival. But here is the truth most people never learn: reading disrupts those patterns and rewires your thinking. Every time you read, you expose your mind to a new voice, a new perspective, a new strategy, a new level of awareness.

You interrupt old narratives and replace them with stronger ones.

This is why people who read consistently think differently. Their minds are trained to stretch instead of shrink, to explore instead of avoid, to question instead of accept, and to see possibility instead of limitation. Reading sharpens your cognitive abilities, your focus, your clarity, your memory, your comprehension, your emotional regulation, and your decision-making. A single book can teach you what took someone else twenty years of failure, experimentation, and recovery to learn. That is what makes reading one of the highest forms of leverage in the world.

Reading also reshapes identity. Every book you absorb becomes part of the internal vocabulary you use to speak to yourself. New words become new beliefs. New insights become new standards. New stories become new mirrors that reflect who you are capable of becoming. Most people struggle not because they lack talent, but because they lack language they do not have words strong enough, clear enough, or powerful enough to guide them toward the future they want. Books fill that gap. Books give you the language of greatness. Books give you the vocabulary of growth. Books give you the blueprint for becoming more.

And when your identity rises, your decisions rise. Your habits rise. Your relationships rise. Your goals rise. Your life rises.

Reading renews your imagination, a tool adults often lose without realizing it. Imagination is not childlike; imagination is vision. It is the ability to dream beyond your present circumstances. It is the ability to see what does not exist yet and move toward it with intention. People who do not read often lose this ability. They stop imagining. They stop dreaming. They stop believing in what could be. Reading restores that inner world. It reminds you that expansion is possible, that transformation is available, and that growth is always within reach.

Reading also strengthens emotional intelligence. When you read, you learn to process emotion, not avoid it. You witness the inner battles of real people, fictional characters, leaders, thinkers, creators, and survivors. You learn the lessons of their failures and the strategies of their victories. You become more empathetic, more self-aware, and more capable of understanding others. Emotional intelligence shapes relationships, leadership, communication, and confidence. And reading is one of the most powerful and underrated ways of developing it.

In every area of life, reading becomes the silent force that separates the average from the exceptional. The average mind is underfed. The exceptional mind is nourished daily. The average person repeats what they know. The exceptional person expands what they know. The average person limits themselves to what their environment taught them. The exceptional person learns from mentors they have never met, minds they have never encountered, and teachers who live through their pages.

Reading does not just inform you. Reading forms you. It molds you into someone wiser, stronger, clearer, more disciplined, more creative, and more capable of building the future you desire. Reading is not just the Sixth Pillar of becoming *B.E.T.T.E.R²*, Reading is the door you walk through to access every greater version of yourself.

## The Five S's of Learning

Most people read for exposure, but very few read for transformation. Years ago, when I was teaching students who struggled to stay focused, stay confident, and stay connected to the material in front of them, I noticed something troubling: they were reading every day, yet remembering almost nothing. I watched bright, capable students try to study, only to become discouraged because the information never seemed to stick. They believed something was wrong with them, when the truth was simple they showed them what to learn but no one had ever shown them how to learn.

One afternoon after class, I stayed behind and asked myself a question that changed everything: *"If students cannot remember what they read, is the problem their ability, or is it the process?"* That one question opened the door to a new discovery. I began experimenting. I watched how they engaged with the page. I paid attention to how they reacted to written words. I studied how the brain absorbs and retains information. And slowly, a pattern revealed itself.

The students who improved the fastest were not the ones who read the most they were the ones who interacted with the reading in multiple ways. They saw it. They said it. They wrote it. They shared it. And they studied it with intention. Their learning expanded because their engagement deepened. That was the moment the Five S's of Learning were born.

What started as a classroom experiment became something far more powerful. The results were undeniable. Grades went up. Confidence rose. Understanding strengthened. Students who once felt defeated by learning started raising their hands again. They remembered more, applied more, and believed more in their own abilities. And from that moment forward, I committed myself to using the Five S's not only to teach academic lessons, but to teach life lessons because the ability to learn faster, deeper, and better is one of the greatest advantages a person can have.

The Five S's became more than a technique. They became a principle for transformation. A strategy for growth. A system for becoming *B.E.T.T.E.R²*. Knowledge only becomes power when it becomes understanding, and understanding only becomes power when it becomes application. To make reading a true pillar of growth, you must train your mind to absorb, retain, and use what you learn. One of the most effective ways to do that is by practicing the Five S's of Learning. It is a simple yet powerful system that strengthens memory, deepens comprehension, and moves information from short-term awareness into long-term wisdom. And once you understand how each "S" works, you will unlock a level of learning that most people never reach. Let us walk through them together. Now let's break down each "S" so you can apply them in your own life and transform the way you learn forever.

The first "S" is **See It**. Take a moment to truly look at the words on the page. Slow down. Let the language land. Visual attention is the first doorway to learning, and most people rush right past it.

The second "S" is **Say It**. Read key lines out loud. When you speak what you read, you activate both sight and sound, two major learning modalities working together. Now the information isn't just in front of you; it's entering you.

The third "S" is **Scribe It**. Write it down in your own words. Writing activates the kinesthetic learning system, the physical, tactile part of the brain that locks memory in place. When your hand moves, your mind remembers.

The fourth "S" is **Share It**. Within the first twelve to twenty-four hours, repeat what you learned to someone else. Teaching instantly strengthens retention. Sharing forces your mind to organize, recall, and articulate the idea which is how it becomes yours.

The fifth "S" is **Study It**. Micro-study the big concepts. Take a quote, a paragraph, or a key idea and put it on a note card or inside your phone. Review it intentionally. Always study with the intention to teach, not the intention to test.

What you study to test goes into short-term memory and disappears. What you study to teach goes into long-term memory and transforms you.

When you practice the 5 S's consistently, reading stops being an activity and becomes a skill, a tool that sharpens your thinking, expands your capacity, and elevates every part of your life.

**THE READ PRACTICE (Action Steps)**

Knowledge rises through intention, consistency, and curiosity. These steps will help you strengthen your mind, expand your perspective, and elevate your life through reading.

## 1. Choose One Book That Matches Your Next Level

Select a book that aligns with the future you are building, not the life you are leaving. Do not choose based on popularity; choose based on purpose. The right book at the right time becomes a mentor, a guide, and a mirror. Begin with one book and commit fully to finishing it.

## 2. Set a Daily Reading Rhythm

Reading becomes powerful when it becomes rhythmic. Choose a consistent daily time ten minutes in the morning, fifteen minutes before bed, or a chapter during lunch. It does not need to be long; it needs to be regular. Consistency builds comprehension, discipline, and momentum.

### 3. Apply the "One Insight Rule"

Every time you read, look for one sentence, one idea, or one concept that elevates your thinking. Write it down. Reflect on it. Use it. When you extract one insight each day, you compound wisdom faster than most people acquire it in a year.

### 4. Create a Reading Environment That Supports Focus

Design a space that quiets your mind: a corner, a chair, a cafe, or a quiet room. Turn off notifications. Silence noise. Protect your attention. Your environment influences your ability to absorb, retain, and apply what you read.

### 5. Track Your Reading Like You Track Your Goals

Growth becomes visible when it is recorded. Keep a simple list of the books you finish. Add the date. Add the biggest lesson. Watching the list grow builds confidence and creates proof of your intellectual evolution.

## 6. Share What You Learn With One Person

Teaching amplifies learning. When you share an insight with someone, a friend, a coworker, a partner you imprint the lesson more deeply into your mind. Wisdom strengthens when it is verbalized and multiplied.

## 7. Replace Ten Minutes of Scrolling With Ten Minutes of Reading

This one habit can change a year of your life. Swap distraction for development. Replace noise with knowledge. Replace consumption with consciousness. Reading is not about finding time; it is about reclaiming time.

## 8. Keep a "Reading-to-Action" Journal

Write down how each book applies to your goals, habits, relationships, mindset, or decisions. Insight without application becomes entertainment. Insight with action becomes transformation. Reading is your blueprint. Use it.

## 9. Revisit One Book Each Year That Changed You

Re-reading a powerful book deepens your understanding and reveals new layers. You are not the same person you were the first time you read it. Returning to a great book strengthens your foundation and renews your discipline.

*"Reinvention begins the moment you refuse to remain who you were and courageously step into who you are becoming."*

— *Sylvester Mayo*

# CHAPTER 7

# REINVENTION

## The Seventh Pillar of Personal Reinvention

*"Reinvention begins the day you stop accepting the version of you that survival created." — Sylvester Mayo*

Reinvention is not about changing who you are. Reinvention is about releasing who you are *no longer willing to be*. It is the choice to rise beyond the version of yourself that life, struggle, fear, pain, and survival forced you to become. Reinvention begins the moment you decide that the future deserves a stronger you, a clearer you, a wiser you, a more disciplined you, and a more powerful you. Reinvention is the point where excuses end and identity evolves.

Most people never reinvent themselves because they are loyal to a version of themselves that no longer matches their vision. They stay attached to old habits, old labels, old beliefs, and old environments because it feels familiar even when it limits them. Familiarity can be more dangerous than failure. Familiarity convinces you to stay the same. Reinvention invites you to become more.

Reinvention is not an event, it is an awakening. It is the point in your life you must eventually arrive at. You do not get there because someone pushes you there, but because life itself prepares you for it. Reinvention comes after the disappointments that shook you, the letdowns that drained you, the patterns that exhausted you, and the cycles that forced you to confront one truth: you can no longer blame people, circumstances, or experiences for where you stand. Reinvention begins the moment you stop pointing outward and start looking inward.

It is the moment you finally tell yourself, "I refuse to shrink for the rest of my life. I refuse to repeat the same year over and over again. I refuse to let the story of my past become the ceiling of my future." Reinvention is a declaration that you are done living life in reaction to what happened to you. It is the turning point where you choose to create what happens *through* you.

Every great transformation begins with a decision. A decision to break cycles. A decision to rise above excuses. A decision to outgrow environments that drain you. A decision to step into the unfamiliar because the unfamiliar is where your future lives. Reinvention is uncomfortable not because you are becoming someone fake, but because you are returning to the version of yourself you were always meant to be.

You cannot become better while protecting the patterns that keep you average. You cannot become stronger while defending the habits that weaken you. You cannot elevate your life while holding onto the same mindset that created your limitations.

> *Reinvention is the courage to walk*
> *away from the version of yourself that*
> *survived and walk toward the version*
> *of yourself that is ready to live.*

Nothing in your life changes until *you* change. Not your circumstances. Not your relationships. Not your opportunities. *You.* Reinvention begins internally long before it manifests externally. A new mindset leads to new decisions. New decisions lead to new habits. New habits lead to new outcomes. Reinvention is the art of replacing the old blueprint with the one you were truly designed for.

Reinvention is not just possible, it is necessary. Without it, you repeat cycles. With it, you create breakthroughs. Without it, you stay stuck in comfort. With it, you rise into calling. Reinvention is the bridge between who you were and who you are becoming. And the only person who can walk across that bridge is you.

## The Moment YOU Decide to Rise

Reinvention begins with awakening, but it becomes real the moment you make a conscious decision to rise. Not tomorrow. Not when life feels easier. Not when fear finally disappears. Reinvention starts the moment you decide that the life you see in your spirit matters more than the life you have been settling for. Every person eventually stands at a crossroad, the life they have been living and the life they were created to become. And that crossroads rarely arrives with fireworks or clarity. It usually comes quietly, in moments of exhaustion, in moments of honesty, in moments when you realize you can no longer pretend that everything is fine. It comes when you feel the internal tug that says, "I cannot keep living the same chapter and calling it a book."

Reinvention happens when something inside you refuses to stay buried. There comes a day when remaining the same becomes more painful than changing. A day when pretending no longer works. A day when ignoring your potential feels like betrayal. A day when you know, deep in your spirit, that if you do not change now, nothing in your life will change later. That is the day reinvention begins not because life suddenly becomes different, but because you finally decide to become different.

Reinvention is not about becoming someone new. It is about becoming who you were always meant to be. It is peeling back the layers of fear, guilt, regret, shame, and limitation that life may have placed on top of you. It is remembering your strength, reclaiming your identity, restoring your confidence, and rebuilding your life from the inside out. Reinvention requires responsibility, the kind that says, "I am not defined by what happened to me; I am defined by what I decide to build from here." It requires courage, the kind that says, "I may not know every step, but I will not stay where I am." It requires surrender, the kind that says, "Not everything from my old life can follow me into my new one." And it requires belief, the kind that says, "My future deserves the best version of me, not the leftover version of me."

More than anything, reinvention requires commitment. You cannot reinvent yourself once and declare the work complete. Reinvention is a lifestyle. You reinvent yourself every time you outgrow your environment. You reinvent yourself every time you outgrow your excuses. You reinvent yourself every time you outgrow your comfort zone. You reinvent yourself every time you outgrow the version of you that settled for less than what you were capable of becoming. Reinvention is evolution done on purpose, not by accident.

This is your reminder that you are allowed to change. You are allowed to grow. You are allowed to rewrite your story. You are allowed to become unrecognizable to the version of you who stayed small for too long. Because becoming *B.E.T.T.E.R².* is not just about improvement it is about rebirth. And the moment you decide to rise, truly rise your entire life begins to rise with you.

## The Day Reinvention Became Non-Negotiable for Me

Years ago, I was an electrician in a major manufacturing company and a good one. A very good one. They called me *The Chairman* because of how well I knew my craft. One day, the company created a brand-new position, it was a joint-venture leadership role between the company and the union to spearhead a major safety initiative. It was a big job, a visible job, a job that would shift the entire direction of my career. And I wanted it.

I mentioned it to a coworker, a man I had personally trained, someone whose skills I helped shape. When I told him I was thinking about applying, he did not just doubt me he laughed. Loud. Hard. Long enough that I felt the insult burn in my chest. Then he said the words that still echo in the back chambers of my mind to this day:

"You think they are going to give *you* that job? YOU? They are just posting it to make it legal. They already know who they are giving that leadership position to."

His words cut deep. But they did not stop me. Because inside, beneath the hurt, was something stronger, a whisper that said, *You can do this. You got this. You belong in that room. Apply anyway.*

So I applied. And as they say the rest is history.

Not only did I get the position, I excelled. I did not just lead the process, I ended up managing three internal processes simultaneously. I built and trained a team of 30 leaders who were responsible for managing the workflow and safety practices of more than 270 employees. After proving consistent success, my responsibilities expanded even further. I became the manager of six additional processes across the United States and collaborated with two more in Canada.

But reinvention did not stop there. I went back to school. Earned two more degrees breaking the barrier of credentials, removing every excuse, and stepping fully into the man I knew I could become.

And today? I travel the world teaching leaders how to grow, improve, transform, and become *B.E.T.T.E.R²*. all because I refused to let someone else's disbelief become the limit of my identity.

Reinvention is not about where you start. Reinvention is about who you decide to become, especially when no one believes you can.

## Becoming the Future You

Reinvention is not just about walking away from an old life; it is about walking toward the life you were always meant to live. The most powerful version of reinvention is not backward-looking, it is forward-leading. It asks a higher question: *Who is the person I am becoming, and what would it look like to live as them today?*

Every person has a "future self", a more disciplined, more courageous, more focused, more fulfilled version of who they are right now. That version of you already exists in potential. It lives in your imagination, your desires, your goals, your quiet moments of clarity, and the internal pull that whispers, "There is more for you." Reinvention is the process of bringing that future self into the present.

To reinvent your life, you must begin by studying the person you aspire to be. What choices does that version of you make? How do they speak? How do they think? What habits do they practice? What standards do they keep? What environments do they seek? What boundaries do they honor? What does their daily life look like?

Reinvention requires you to start acting like that future version of yourself *before* you feel ready. Identity does not shift after change identity shifts before change. The life you want cannot arrive while you are still behaving like the person who is not ready for it.

The future you is not a stranger you must discover; it is the real you that you must remember. The real you who was courageous before fear crept in. The real you who was curious before doubt clouded your mind. The real you who was bold before life taught you to shrink. Reinvention is not becoming someone "different." It is returning to someone deeper the version of you that life tried to bury, silence, or distract.

This is the turning point most people never reach: the moment when you stop living from memory and start living from imagination. Memory is who you have been. Imagination is who you are becoming. Memory keeps you safe. Imagination makes you powerful. Memory repeats the past. Imagination designs the future.

The people who transform their lives do one simple thing consistently, they wake up each day and behave as if the future version of themselves is already here. They speak like that version. They think like that version. They plan like that version. They show up like that version. They choose like that version. Every day becomes a rehearsal for the life they are building.

And slowly, the line between who they are and who they are becoming begins to disappear. The future self becomes the current self. Reinvention becomes identity. Identity becomes lifestyle. Lifestyle becomes destiny.

Reinvention is not about what you have been through; it is about what you are walking into. It is not about your history; it is about your horizon. The life you want is not waiting for a better day, it is waiting for a better you. And that version of you is already within reach. Reinvention is the bridge.

Reinvention is not a finish line, it is a decision you make every single day. It is the quiet commitment to rise again, to adjust again, to believe again, and to become again. Reinvention begins the moment you stop accepting the version of yourself shaped by old habits, old fears, old stories, and old choices and start embracing the version shaped by clarity, purpose, courage, and intention. You are not defined by what happened before this chapter; you are defined by what you choose after it. And now that you have learned the pillars Belief, Energy, Talent, Time, Support, and Reading you have everything you need to build a life that is stronger, clearer, richer, and more aligned with the future you desire. Reinvention is the moment you declare, "I refuse to go back to who I was, because I am committed to becoming *B.E.T.T.E.R²*." Better is not just a word in this book it is the new identity you step into. It is who you are becoming next. And that journey begins now.

## THE REINVENTION PRACTICE (Action Steps)

Reinvention isn't a wish. It's a discipline. These steps will help you actively shift into the next version of yourself, the version you've been growing toward throughout this entire book.

### 1. Identify the One Pattern You Must Release

Reinvention begins with honesty. Identify one habit, one belief, one behavior, or one cycle that is keeping you tied to who you used to be. Write it down. This is the version of you that can no longer come with you into your future.

### 2. Define the New Identity You Are Becoming

Write a clear declaration of who you want to be from this moment forward. "I am a person who…" Fill in the sentence with the identity you are choosing, not the one life handed you. Identity drives action; action creates reinvention.

### 3. Choose One Daily Ritual That Supports the New You

Reinvention requires repetition. Select one small daily act that aligns with the version of you that you are becoming something you can do consistently to reinforce your transformation. Morning gratitude, reading 10 minutes a day, setting a daily intention, journaling, or an evening reflection. One ritual can change everything.

## 4. Remove One Thing That Drains You

Reinvention requires subtraction as much as addition. Remove one thing that weakens you: a distraction, a toxic conversation, a draining environment, or a commitment that no longer aligns with your growth. Every time you remove what weakens you, you create space for what strengthens you.

## 5. Add One Form of Support You Have Avoided

Reinvention should never be done alone. Choose one supportive connection you need: mentorship, community, accountability, coaching, or partnership. The next version of you requires the right voices around you. Add them intentionally.

## 6. Reinforce Your Reinvention with Reading

Choose one book each month that supports the identity you're building. Reading is how you rewire your thoughts, deepen your wisdom, and strengthen the new foundation you now stand on. Better thinking creates a Better you.

## 7. End Each Day with the "Better Reflection"

Before bed, ask yourself: "What did I do today that made me better?" Even one small improvement is progress. Reinvention is built brick by brick, decision by decision, day by day.

Reinvention is not the final step; it is the commitment to never return to who you were once you have learned better. Throughout this journey, you have walked through the complete *B.E.T.T.E.R²* framework, not as a theory to admire but as a way of life to embody. You have examined your belief and learned that nothing in your life rises until your belief does. You have learned to guard and elevate your energy, understanding that how you show up determines how far you go. You have discovered your talent, not as something you wait to be chosen for, but as something you develop through discipline and courage. You have learned to honor time, not by asking for more of it, but by becoming more intentional with what you already have. You have learned to enlist the right people, recognizing that growth was never meant to be a solo journey. You have learned to read, to expand your thinking, sharpen your wisdom, and feed your future. And now, through reinvention, you have been reminded of the most powerful truth of all: you are not broken, you are becoming.

Reinvention does not require rejecting your past; it requires refusing to let your past limit your future. It is the decision to honor the lessons without reliving the pain, to extract wisdom without carrying the weight. It is the moment you accept responsibility for who you are becoming next. The greatest mistake people make after growth is returning to familiarity. They finish the work, feel inspired, and slowly drift back into old patterns, old environments, and old excuses. But you now know better. And once you know better, you are responsible for becoming better. *B.E.T.T.E.R²* is not a phase, a season, or a moment of motivation. It is a lifestyle. It is the daily practice of thinking intentionally, choosing deliberately, and responding to life with awareness and purpose.

There will be days when you feel strong and days when you feel stretched. There will be moments of clarity and moments of uncertainty. Reinvention does not promise ease; it promises alignment. It means you no longer abandon yourself when life applies pressure. Instead, you pause, reflect, realign, and rise again. The power of this framework is not found in reading it once, but in returning to it often. Each time your belief wavers, you return to belief. Each time your energy drops, you protect and restore it. Each time your talent feels dormant, you train it. Each time time feels scarce, you refocus your priorities. Each time you feel isolated, you enlist support. Each time your thinking feels limited, you read and expand your mind. And each time life forces change, you reinvent instead of retreat. This is how growth becomes permanent.

You are no longer waiting for permission. You are no longer waiting for the right moment. You are no longer waiting to be chosen. You are choosing. Choosing to live intentionally. Choosing to rise responsibly. Choosing to become who you were always capable of becoming. *B.E.T.T.E.R²* does not end here; it begins every morning you wake up and decide to live aligned with what you now know. And from this point forward, whenever life asks you who you are becoming, you already have the answer. You are becoming *B.E.T.T.E.R².*

For more information, coaching, speaking
or bookings scan the QR Code below
or visit www.sylvestermayo.com

www.ingramcontent.com/pod-product-compliance
Lightning Source LLC
Chambersburg PA
CBHW020739130626
46554CB00006B/2061

*9 7 9 8 9 9 2 5 3 5 9 7 6 *